THE SCIENCE OF

BASKETBALL

By

William Anthony

PLAY
SMART

BookLife
PUBLISHING

©2019
BookLife Publishing Ltd.
King's Lynn
Norfolk PE30 4LS
All rights reserved.
Printed in Malaysia.

A catalogue record for this book is available from the British Library.

ISBN: 978-1-78637-655-8

Written by:
William Anthony

Edited by:
Emilie Dufresne

Designed by:
Gareth Liddington

Photocredits:

Cover – glenda, Monkey Business Images, Torsak Thammachote, naito29, FocusStocker, artproem, 2 – Fernando Cruz, 4 – LDWYTN, 5 – Monkey Business Images, 6 – Alex Kravtsov, 7 – GotziLA STOCK, 8 – Ebitkar, 9 – oneinchpunch, 10 – Phovoir, 11 – Ivica Drusany, 12 – Petur Asgeirsson, 13 – Yuriy Golub, 14 – Boris Ryaposov, 15 – icsnaps, 17 – Trong Nguyen, 18 – OSTILL is Franck Camhi, 19 – oneinchpunch, 20 – Ljupco Smokovski, 21 – Gino Santa Maria, Yuriy Golub, Nicholas Piccillo.

Images are courtesy of Shutterstock.com. With thanks to Getty Images, Thinkstock Photo and iStockphoto.

All facts, statistics, web addresses and URLs in this book were verified as valid and accurate at time of writing. No responsibility for any changes to external websites or references can be accepted by either the author or publisher.

CONTENTS

Words that look like **this** can be found in the glossary on page 24.

GET ON THE COURT!

Are you ready to learn all about the **forces**, angles and patterns behind basketball? Then lace up your high-tops and grab the ball: the game is about to start!

Basketball is a game where two teams of five players compete against each other to score points. Points are scored by shooting the ball through the hoop that each team is attacking.

HOOP

ATTACKER

Shots made near the basket are worth two points, shots made from behind the three-point line are worth three.

DEFENDER

DIRECT DRIBBLING

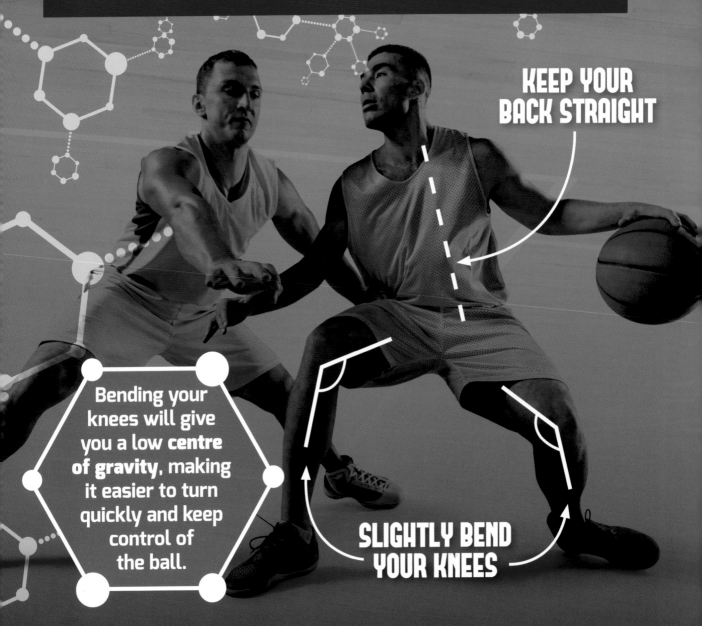

KEEP YOUR BACK STRAIGHT

Bending your knees will give you a low **centre of gravity**, making it easier to turn quickly and keep control of the ball.

SLIGHTLY BEND YOUR KNEES

When your team start to attack, you'll be dribbling from one end of the court to the other. You do this by bouncing the ball on the ground beside you as you travel forward.

In basketball, you must bounce the ball when you are moving around the court. When you bounce the ball, you push it towards the ground. When the ball hits the floor, it **compresses** and rebounds back upwards into your hand.

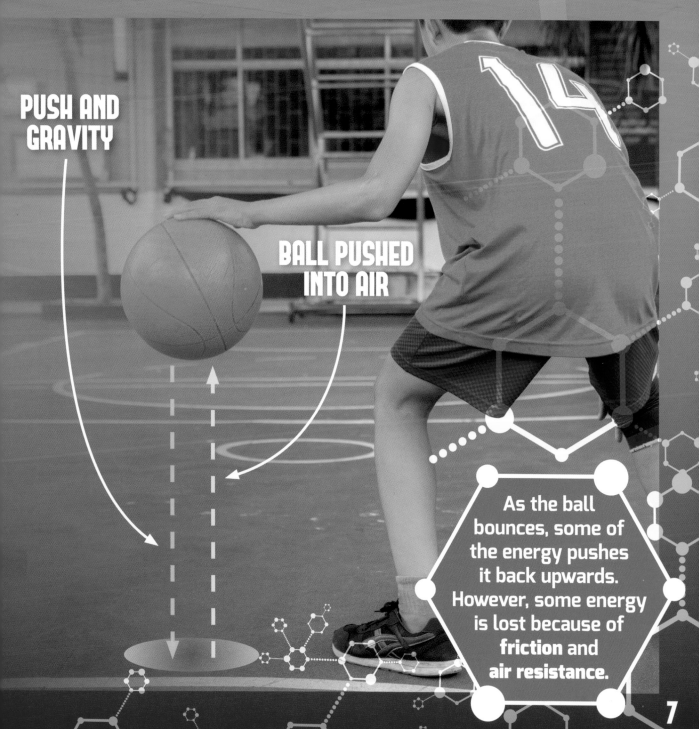

PUSH AND
GRAVITY

BALL PUSHED
INTO AIR

As the ball bounces, some of the energy pushes it back upwards. However, some energy is lost because of **friction** and **air resistance**.

BRILLIANT BOUNCE PASS

If you have an **opponent** marking you, a bounce pass to get the ball to another player might be a good choice. This is when you bounce the ball off the ground to your teammate.

SMALLER ANGLE FOR A CLOSER TEAMMATE

If your teammate is close by, bounce the ball at a smaller angle. If your teammate is farther away the angle will need to be bigger.

To pass to a teammate farther away, you will need to put more force into your pass to make sure it has enough energy to reach them.

BIGGER ANGLE FOR A TEAMMATE FARTHER AWAY

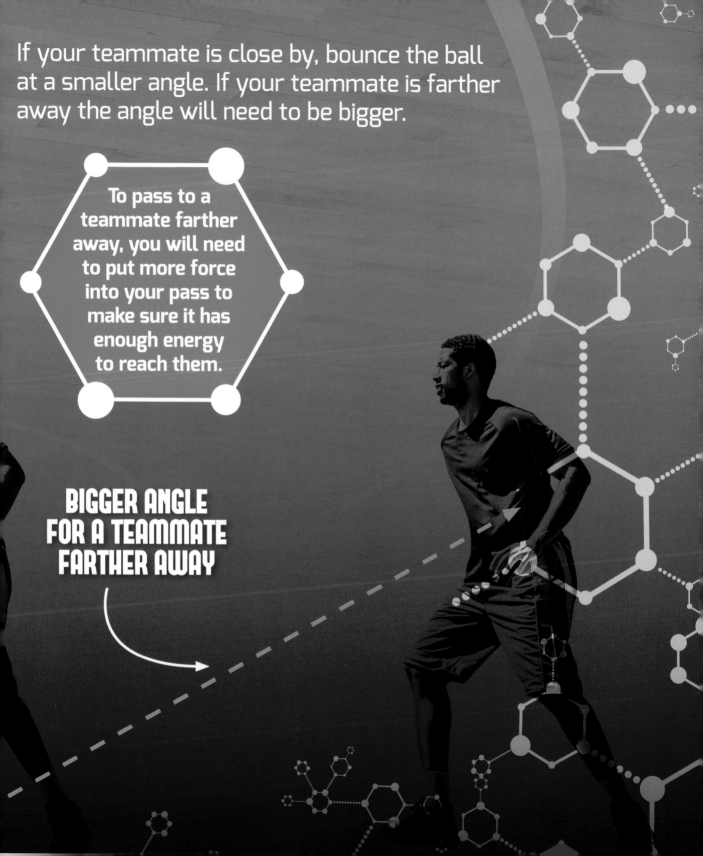

CHEST PASS CHAMPION

If there are no opponents between you and your teammate, you could try a chest pass. Chest passes are normally more **accurate** than bounce passes.

To play a chest pass, bend your elbows and hold the ball near your chest, then push the ball away from you.

BALL NEXT TO CHEST

BENT ELBOWS

EYES

Extend your arms as much as you can to increase the speed of your chest pass.

The more you bend your elbows, the more **potential energy** you create. When you push the ball to make the pass, the potential energy is transferred from your arms into the ball, making it move towards your teammate.

FANCY FOOTWORK

If the player has both hands on the ball, they have to stand still.

PIVOT FOOT

It's hard to make a pass when you're surrounded by defenders. To get out of trouble, you can keep one foot on the ground, and spin around on the spot with the other. This is called **pivoting**.

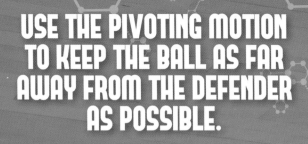

USE THE PIVOTING MOTION TO KEEP THE BALL AS FAR AWAY FROM THE DEFENDER AS POSSIBLE.

Defenders will make big shapes with their bodies to block an attacker's move.

PIVOT FOOT

You can move your free foot round to the left or to the right to get around a defender.

SHARP SHOOTING

When you get close enough to your opponents' hoop, it's time to take a shot. There are lots of shapes and angles that go into the perfect shot.

BEND YOUR SHOOTING ARM INTO TWO RIGHT ANGLES, ONE AT YOUR ELBOW AND ONE AT YOUR WRIST, AS IF YOU WERE TRYING TO MAKE THREE SIDES OF A SQUARE.

LOOK UPWARDS AND FORWARDS TOWARDS THE HOOP.

YOUR ARM SHOULD LOOK LIKE A SWAN'S NECK!

PUSHING UP WITH YOUR KNEES HELPS TO FORCE THE BALL HIGH INTO THE AIR.

Jumping pushes you high into the air.

After you've taken aim, push up from your knees and extend your arm into a long, straight line. Just as you release the ball, flick your hand towards the hoop to make the ball move forwards.

OFF THE BACKBOARD

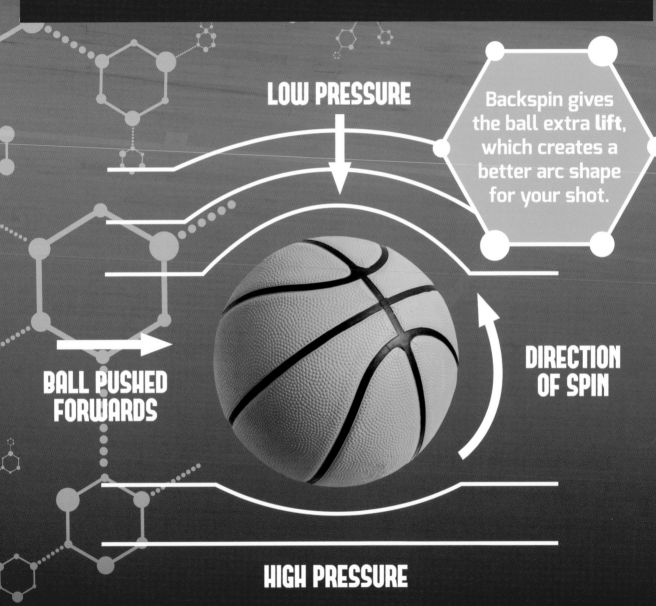

LOW PRESSURE

Backspin gives the ball extra **lift**, which creates a better arc shape for your shot.

BALL PUSHED FORWARDS

DIRECTION OF SPIN

HIGH PRESSURE

When you flick your wrist towards the board during your shot, you will put backspin on the ball. This creates an area of low **air pressure** above the ball, and high air pressure below it.

When the basketball hits the backboard, the backspin helps the ball to drop down through the hoop, rather than bouncing away.

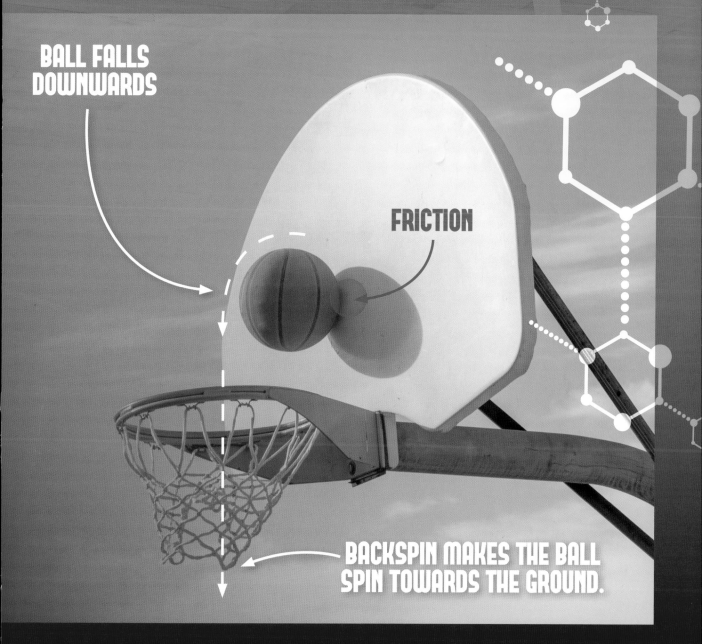

BALL FALLS DOWNWARDS

FRICTION

BACKSPIN MAKES THE BALL SPIN TOWARDS THE GROUND.

When the ball touches the backboard, friction is created. The backspin and the energy lost through friction make the ball fall downwards.

DEADLY DEFENCE

Keeping your knees bent gives you potential energy, meaning you are always ready to jump, move or block a shot.

DEFENDER

ATTACKER

When your team is defending, your task is to stop the attacking team working their way towards the hoop and scoring points. Just like when you're attacking, keeping a low centre of gravity is important.

When you're trying to stop your opponent from passing or shooting, making yourself into a big shape will make it harder for them. Spread your arms out wide and separate your feet to cover a big area.

OPEN ARMS OUT WIDE

STAND WITH FEET APART

Making a big shape with your body gives the attacker less space to pass or move into.

WHAT'S NEXT?

When you're defending, guessing your opponent's next move will help you make a block. Thinking like an attacker will help you defend their next move.

Take a look at this attacker. If you were defending against her, what position would you get into?

Would it be position 1, 2, or 3? Remember to think about whether she is getting ready to make a chest pass, a bounce pass, or take a shot.

MAKE THE BLOCK

That's right, it's position 2. Get ready to jump and stretch your arms, because she's about to shoot! Let's take a look at the science behind the shot.

DIRECTION

Her eyes are looking upwards and forwards. This means she is probably looking towards the hoop in front of her. Position 1 is too low to stop this shot, it would be more suited to blocking bounce passes.

ANGLES

Her arms are starting to make right angles. This means she is getting ready to take a shot. Position 2 is perfect for jumping high in the air and blocking the ball!

ENERGY

Her knees are bent, so she is storing potential energy which will help her jump. This means you're going to have to jump too if you want to block her shot! Position 3 is good, but you won't be high enough in the air to stop her from scoring!

IT'S VERY IMPORTANT TO LOOK AT YOUR OPPONENT WHEN PLAYING, AND NOT JUST THE BALL. THIS IS CALLED "PLAYING THE PLAYER, AND NOT THE BALL".

GLOSSARY

accurate	precise and careful
air pressure	the force air puts on any surface in contact with it
air resistance	the frictional force air creates against a moving object
centre of gravity	the point at which the weight of something is balanced
compresses	squeezes something using pressure
forces	pushes or pulls on an object
friction	when one object rubs against another
lift	an upward force
opponent	a member of another team playing against you
pivoting	turning around a fixed point
potential energy	the amount of energy stored inside an object that is ready to be used

INDEX